I0414828

Advertitis™

THE CREATIVE CLINICIANS™

AuthorHouse™
1663 Liberty Drive
Bloomington, IN 47403
www.authorhouse.com
Phone: 1-800-839-8640

©2010 The Creative Clinicians™. All rights reserved.

No part of this book may be reproduced, stored in a retrieval system, or
transmitted by any means without the written permission of the author.

First published by AuthorHouse   6/5/2010

ISBN: 978-1-4520-0017-6 (hc)
ISBN: 978-1-4520-0016-9 (sc)
ISBN: 978-1-4520-0015-2 (e)

Library of Congress Control Number: 2010905728

Printed in the United States of America
Bloomington, Indiana

This book is printed on acid-free paper.

Designed by Elena Thomson

"When my eyes don't know where to go, my mind knows they're headed nowhere."

The Creative Clinicians™

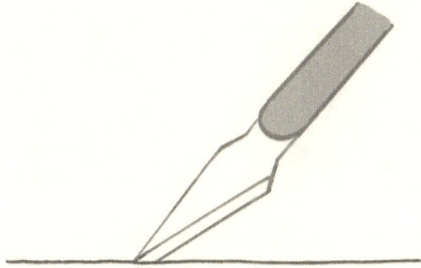

Someone has to make the first cut on the cadaver and the Creative Clinicians have done it with precision. Dissecting the pharmaceutical advertising business and marketing communication, they go below the skin, into the anatomy and physiology. They present not only an internal retrospection on how the creative message irrevocably breaks down through wayward opinion or compliment cascade, but in the process offer invaluable insight and practical tools in which to remedy the situation and remain compliant in an ever-changing healthcare system. This is a refreshing dialogue for today's marketing and communication challenges.

This book contains key insights and valuable tools.

To Elena, Eva and Stella Mae.

Contents

Birth of a notion.

1

Advertitis™ is by no means a bona fide medical term. In fact, until the conception of this book, it didn't even exist. However, you may be surprised to learn Advertitis is not only highly contagious – it's worryingly widespread throughout the world of pharmaceutical advertising. What is Advertitis? And exactly why is it something we should be so concerned about?

One not so extraordinary day, a medical director was watching his creative director deliver a short, albeit pithy, presentation. The compelling demonstration showed how a powerful, single-minded advertisement could, through off-hand cursory remarks and ill thought-out opinions, quickly develop into a perplexing mess of tangled messages. The creative moral seemed simple enough. However, through the medical director's eyes, a very different story was being told. The creative director's few PowerPoint® slides weren't so much describing the gradual communication *breakdown* of a world-renowned advertisement but the gradual *inflammation* of extremely delicate tissue. To the physician the swelling was the result of an infiltration of a multitude of unrelated opinions that were infecting and beginning to tear the *tissue* beyond all recognition. The fact that an advertising concept is often called a tissue during the early stages of development made the medical director's observation all the more astute. Further discussion exposed and then centered on a disturbing truth. Today's pharmaceutical advertising is in the most fundamental sense an often-confusing mix of messages and claims with little priority in terms of importance. You only have to flip through the pages of *JAMA* to see how challenging many ads can be to decipher. It's not uncommon to witness half a dozen messages screaming at you at once. A place where clichéd happy smiling patients, animals on skateboards and the ubiquitous boxing gloves all scrap for attention. Few ads cleanly state in a memorable manner one single differentiating claim — a real life-and-death state of affairs in a highly competitive and crowded marketplace.

As the creative and medical partners began to debate the reasons for this fundamental communication breakdown, they also questioned how they could buck the negative trend in a consistent manner. Undoubtedly, in many cases, ever-stricter regulatory guidance, limitations and mandates often temper the creative solution and completely suffocate any compelling communication. Obviously these layers won't disappear so the real challenge is to work within this complexity and penetrate the dense set of constrictions. The partners came to the conclusion that the conception and development of single-minded creative ideas rely on several critical factors: The creative has to be rooted and grounded in the medical and scientific rigor of the product and disease state. It has to be synthesized into a compelling, simple vision. To bring this into effect both creative and medical have to be joined at the hip every step of the way – not just by a cursory dialogue at the start of the project and then again at the end. Both concluded that without an innate connection between the two skills sets, truly compelling, medically relevant creative solutions would continue to be elusive. Without the insights into the minds of physicians, patients and customers, you can't take full advantage.

In many cases it is, at best, a piecemeal process, fragmented with no real consistency. Perhaps if a definitive set of criteria were proposed and adhered to, then every tissue would have the opportunity to thrive into a powerful piece of communication. The authors clearly believe this is the case and to reflect this important alliance they propose new titles be given to all creative and medical directors. It's the reason why the authors choose to call themselves *Creative Clinicians*.

A case study.

2

I was called to an emergency by my staff to respond to a serious incident that needed my immediate attention. When I arrived all was utter chaos. Confusion and disorientation swept through the room as many bystanders looked on this very tragic and traumatic scene.

I tried to get as much history as possible, rapidly and efficiently, from those huddled together amidst the panic. It became clear that there had been considerable past history of this type of presentation before.

As I focused on the task at hand, it was immediately apparent that the victims were unresponsive and motionless, barely hanging on to dear life. I quickly assessed vital signs that revealed a weak and thready pulse, shallow breathing and extremely elevated pressures. Reflexes were exceptionally blunted, central cognition was impaired and posturing was setting in among those affected. Amidst all this commotion, I suddenly noticed the horrific sight of exposed tissue that was severely inflamed and damaged beyond recognition. The body of tissue was grossly compromised: extremely friable, and swollen with obvious distortion.

I immediately requested a number of stat consults and began securing central lines to the victims. In the end, after reviewing the findings on physical examination, incorporating relevant history and expert opinion from a number of consults, I determined that the victims were suffering from a severe case of what we call . . . moderate to severe Advertitis.

3

Advertitis™ (in case you were wondering), is not just a silly name for a book. 'Itis' by its very definition means inflammation. The condition occurs anywhere in the human body, be it an organ, tissue, joint or a nail. Dermatitis, for example, is the inflammation of the skin's dermal layer. Appendicitis is the inflammation of the appendix. Therefore in the minds of the Creative Clinicians, no word is more appropriate. Advertitis is defined thus: *the inflammation of the creative tissue, which over time swells losing its integrity and purpose, due to external forces.* Instead of simplicity, it's toxicity. In place of compelling, is swelling. The visceral reaction of the by-standing team in the previous case study is typically how customers react to the majority of published pharmaceutical advertisements (eliciting no response, thready pulse and hardly breathing). Right from the onset, opinion after opinion completely transfigures the delicate, native creative tissue. Every subsequent well-intended compliment (internally at the advertising agency and then externally at the client end) rips and tears the delicate structure, making it friable (bleeds easily) and unable to withstand scrutiny and pushback.

The Big Four

Typically, a physician defines inflammation by indicators known as the big four: rubor, calor, tumor, and dolor (red, hot, swollen, and painful.) A fifth sign of chronic inflammation called *functio laesa,* literally translated means dysfunctional tissue or organ. This is the point of no return as all sense of purpose is lost. Similarly, as opinions and conjecture attack the creative tissue, they display the very components or signs of acute inflammation. No longer are the creative tissues robust, full of valor, humor, and color. The Creative Clinician's equate several (though not inclusive) qualities to compelling concepts.. They believe the trigger for this inflammatory process in creative tissues is two-fold:

1) Initially, because a best practice process is not followed routinely, there is a lack of compliance or poor use of the tools available to help guide the creative work.

2) The driving force behind this is a cascade of compliments. Inherent in the physiologic process of creative tissue mutation is the sequence of mediators or

compliments that drive inflammation.

The Compliment Cascade

The *complement cascade,* (in medical terms), draws some interesting parallels with the creative evaluation process. These are the very inflammatory factors that amplify response and activation of tissue-killing defense mechanisms, or cascade. In other words, here is a built-in, innate defense mechanism (a double meaning if you will), that both recognizes and subsequently binds to infectious/contaminated components or insult driving inflammation. Go figure! Okay, let's apply this hair-brained biological methodology to advertising. Anyone working in pharmaceutical marketing will testify to the frustration, systematic push back, and various immovable stances taken by all stakeholders. This slow, progressive infectious process inflames the creative tissue to such a degree that the very integrity of the idea is lost. Only until the tissue contains everyone's ideas – and conversely no one's – is agreement "reached" (with a huge collective sigh of relief!). This end result, however, is rarely a happy median.

The detail that goes into saying nothing.

4

So let's go back to the beginning. The creative tissue, a beautifully crafted yet simple idea starts life as no more than a sketch and a few words on paper. If it's truly a great idea it will eventually have the ability to engage the minds of millions and drive them to purchase the advertised product. A tissue drawn out for the first time is an exciting moment because at this precise instant it has infinite potential. Here lies the competitive edge – the creative means to outmaneuver and defeat the competition.

Once the creative team has landed on several concepts an internal presentation is held. For the first time the tissue is open and exposed to the environment that lies outside of the incubation unit – the creative office. In these vulnerable moments of life, the tissue, newly conceived is proffered up to an assembled agency audience of varying backgrounds. This is the single most important meeting in the life of a tissue because this is the moment in which it will either thrive or, as is often the case, be subjected to highly invasive and extremely wide-ranging deliberation. A whole multi factor of influencers – or compliment cascade – will descend on the single-minded thought. If the forthcoming discussions and opinions are not managed in a way that enables the idea to grow and flourish, the body of the tissue will quickly be attacked, becoming compromised and inflamed. As contamination persists, so the tissue continues to lose all integrity as debate, positioning of opinion and posturing all kick in. With the inflammation and compliment cascade in full force, defense mechanisms, compromised positions, barter and negotiation all take precedence over the creative evaluation. Remarkably, even the creative team, whose concepts they are, is wide now open to change. There is now an almost frantic need to make the concepts *more correct*. In fact, making the concepts *more correct* has become the whole goal! *We're almost there . . . a few more tweaks . . .hey, we're on a roll!* Sound familiar?

Of course, many more rounds of debating and postulating are assured. Agency, client and the subsequent cycle of research will all continue in their quest to make the concepts *more correct*. So by the time it reaches the hallowed glossy interiors of the medical journals it'll be a perplexing mess of countless message points. Paralysis from the headline down, eyebrows, subheads and tag lines will grapple for the reader's attention. Eyeballs will juggle with an information overload. It's new, it's improved, it's longer lasting, it's almost always the #1 physician prescribed and of course it provides the tolerability patients need and the efficacy they deserve. Now void of sensation. it reads like an epitaph rather than an advertisement. This is the detail that goes into saying nothing.

The silent killer.

5

Never shy of an analogy, the Creative Clinicians present one that truly bats the proverbial ball out of the legendary park. Looking closely at this slow, incendiary pathology they discovered a profound parallel with an equally inflammatory viral infection called chronic Hepatitis C (HCV). Here the smoldering process damages the liver tissue, distorts and scars the architecture and ultimately affects the overall functionality of the liver. In many instances, it's not known where, how or when the actual infection arose. Yet due to its nature, the course of illness is nearly always protracted. Often those affected don't know it for decades. The very same signals and red flags that are the hallmarks of chronic HCV infection are central to the briefing, conception and subsequent evaluation of the creative concept. Silent, slow, progressive tissue damage which over time continues to impede the intended communication.

Of course, the liver is, by its very nature pretty resilient in terms of function. This is because it has a lot of reserve, bags of capacity. Incredibly, 75% of the liver could be knocked out before its function even begins to be compromised. Unfortunately, by then enough damage has occurred that cognition becomes impaired and confusion holds sway. This is encephalopathy associated with end stage liver disease, where circulating toxins run unfiltered and create havoc through the system. Inevitably, the sufferer becomes more and more confused as toxins and waste products circulate unfiltered and unchecked as functionality continues to fade. The sufferer is thinking, *I don't understand what you're saying. I don't understand what it is I'm not doing.* In this case, the organ has been chronically injured to the point of dysfunction readily seen as confusion. Communication is irrevocably compromised and impaired.

The Broca's and Wernicke's Advertisements

The classic medical description of compromised communication is aphasia (loss or impairment of comprehending words or processing communication) and is commonly divided into two specific types related to the area of the brain tissue affected. The first is Broca's aphasia, an expressive aphasia, where the sufferers have every intention of expressing themselves, want to say something, but cannot perform the actual output of communication. The other is Wernicke's aphasia, a receptive aphasia, where they are able to say all kinds of things but in no coherent order. None of it makes any sense whatsoever. They confabulate. They talk gibberish. Interestingly, both types of aberrant communication are the result of severely damaged inflamed tissue that draws some interesting parallels within marketing. The Creative Clinicians have termed this atypical marketing communication as *creative aphasia.* This new nomenclature has in turn been broken down into two types: 1) The *Broca's advertisement,* where the reaction is that the ad says absolutely nothing to the observer or customer; 2) The *Wernicke's advertisement* where the ad is saying innumerable things but none of what's being said hangs together. There's nothing receptive at all. It's like a word salad – all chopped up and thrown together. In both cases, the result is an inability to communicate the simple single-minded message. You can test this theory by flipping through a few medical journals. Very quickly you'll discover that many so-called communications are simply not fulfilling their purpose.

High-Risk Lifestyle

So, what are the causative factors for creative aphasia? Who are the guilty parties? Can it be quarantined? Is it even curable? Again, the answer can be found in the chronic HCV analogy. Chronic HCV is a viral infection and insult to the organ that can be due to a risky lifestyle or a life of indiscretion, (what physician's call indiscretions of youth). Pharmaceutical marketing often practices in a fragmented, splintered way, and while there are tools or other systematic ways to ensure quality control rarely are they being used in the most effective manner. Is the correct dialogue happening at the beginning of the process? Are the processes and the tools being used in a judicious manner? If not, it's simply system du jour. And that's risky. In essence, this is analogous with the high-risk lifestyle chronic HCV patients tend to lead. How many get liver disease? How many know how or where they contracted it? Well guess what? Those that contract HCV commonly have a high-risk lifestyle, often unclean needles, and drug abuse – hanging with dodgy crowds. Admittedly, there are others who contract HCV who don't have this lifestyle as a risk factor but it's a lower percentage. Fundamentally, the risk increases when you are not following good, healthy practices.

Similarly, this is true in pharmaceutical advertising. Many times, an advertising agency will present a large volume of concepts to their client hoping there is one they will like. (Who on either the client or agency side have not gone through round after painstaking round of conceptualization only for the process to begin again?) In this instance a little therapeutic intervention will go a long way. If you haven't some framework of protective immunity then anyone can attack your creative tissue. By implementing therapeutic intervention, or best practice processes that can be easily adhered to, you guarantee cellular and tissue immunity.

If we look back over the last twenty-five or thirty years we can see this inflammatory viral process has infected an extremely important organ – the pharmaceutical advertising industry. Similarly to chronic HCV where the organ is damaged before any outward signs are recognized, the processes within pharmaceutical advertising have slowly, over time, been damaging the functionality of its communications. The huge advertising reserve that has been able to withstand a multitude of problems over a long period has come to a breaking point. There are fewer emotive, thought-provoking, insightful ideas emerging. Predictability is preferred over originality. Again and again the tendency is to fall back on the expected, the clichéd generic solutions that have run for other products and are so easily adaptable. (Tear the drug logotype from the bottom right hand corner of any advertisement and then ask a co-worker what the ad is for. It's a deceptively simple exercise that quickly reveals how much of our resources have been exhausted).

Our dysfunctional industrial organ has slowly but surely become damaged over several decades. Well, now it's time for change. Look at how medical care has dramatically changed in the dimensions that influence where we're headed — it's ever evolving — from managed care, scientific advancement and biologic therapies to genetic variations and personalized medicine. Time has come to change our marketing communication strategy. The big question is how are we going to make sure the creative solution embraces the challenges within healthcare so it resonates with where we're going?

Harley Street
meets
SESAME STREET.

6

If we believe that any successful pharmaceutical creative concept is a meld of medical relevance and creative interpretation, we need to examine the relationship between the two practices. In truth, they're a bit of an odd couple. On the one hand you have the medical expert, someone who knows every pathway of every disease, the mechanisms of action, metabolism excretion and the pharmacokinetics and pharmacodynamics of therapeutic agents – they know all those things. And on the other hand you have the creative expert, a lateral thinker, bit of an odd ball, lover of insightful observation and award-winning concepts. In the creative mind, originality is key, and the compelling truth is told in no more than a handful of words.

Let's just pause for a moment to visualize this dynamic. These are two entirely different mindsets, you might even say polar opposites. Yet there they stand on one team with a single objective. It's a bit like Harley Street meets Sesame Street. In the highly specialized world of medicine, one that's constantly evolving in the advancement of disease, it's critical they work side by side. Dry factual information does not and never will lead to fertile ideation. So how often is the physician at the creative side to ensure those great ideas and concepts are being synthesized enough to fully realize this powerful dynamic? How often does he or she provide or ignite medically inspired creative?

Many times an MD, or medical director isn't around. They're part of another division or department, perhaps even in another city. Or else they're a consultation service where the agency will get X number of hours. In short, there's precious little daily or routine connection. These splintered intermittent time frames will undoubtedly begin to infect the friable tissue (not to mention get under the skin of creative). Another important point to mention is that physicians are trained in medical school to be the all-knowing. When it comes to patient or family issues, they're the smartest person around. They know everything – just ask one! They certainly don't like to be challenged – it doesn't go down well. In this situation, the physician is God-like. They possess a God-like complex of *what I say goes. I'm in control. I'm in power.* When they walk into a room, they're often thinking: *You are below me. You don't deserve a lot of my time.* However, as soon they step into the pharmaceutical marketing world, guess what? They're not in power – they're not the one who knows everything. In fact they know less than everyone else. Perhaps it's not surprising – many medical and scientific directors work on a part-time basis so they don't understand the physiology of the industry. Switching from the all-knowing to the need-to-learn is a daunting task. How many physician-cum-marketers intuitively think, *I've embedded myself in the process and jumped in to experience the creative world.* More than likely you'll hear; *don't ask me to change me – in fact I don't need to change me. I'm changing you because I'm the one directing the traffic here.* Rather paradoxically, the physician who committed to life-long learning doesn't apply these noble values to marketing. We need them to ask, *how do I prevent Advertitis?* The simple answer, of course, is that operating alone will never cure it. For example, without the assistance of a radiologist to give the physician needed information, success will continue to be elusive. The same is true in advertising.

White Coat Creative Tension

To help picture the medical and creative dynamic, the Creative Clinicians have drawn on the doctor / patient relationship. Imagine the patient nervously waiting for the doctor's return with those all-important test results, bracing him or herself for the worse. *What will the doctor do? What will they tell me?* They know one thing's for sure – it can't be good news. Unfortunately it's no easier for the physician who knows they're creating anxiety by their mere presence, background and place in society. This situation leads to a patient experiencing a condition called white coat hypertension, or white coat syndrome – a physiologic response to intense anticipation and anxiety; a phenomenon where patients become hypertensive in the clinical setting.. It's a common term among physicians who recognize that patients with hypertension worsen and patients who are normotensive become hypertensive – even when they're adhering to the most rigorous regimen!

Witness the same reaction as the creative team waits for the medical expert to enter the meeting room. Predictably creative will already have a mindset about a medical expert, who more often than not weighs in at the eleventh hour, when the concept is due to be presented to the client the next day. As medical walks through the door the creative team start to break a sweat and their blood pressure rockets. Very soon all those present will be blinded with science. *I don't get it. That metabolic pathway isn't exactly that - it goes this way and it goes that way.* This throws creative into turmoil. They're thinking to themselves: *Where were you when I needed your help? I asked the question weeks ago but haven't heard a thing since.*

Time and again this is where the process breaks down. It's a negative physiologic reaction, likely on both sides in all fairness; physicians are frequently frustrated to have such conversations and may not even have the skills to communicate in a simple, compelling fashion to entrenched creatives who need to open up to new possibilities. Both creative an medical need to set expectations together, understand the past and develop a way of communicating as one solid partnership. Physicians are professionally trained to prevent all kinds of syndromes, yet here they are creating one! They need to realize what creative is expecting of them, creatives anxieties and what physicians have typically represented in the past.

Creative Bedside Manner.

Mastering patient communication is as much an art form as creative advertising. Physicians deal with patients who are at all levels of education. Taking the time and having the patience and verbal skills to communicate clinical status, prognosis, and often difficult and devastating information is crucial to strengthening a genuine patient/physician relationship. This is known as *bedside manner* and in physicians good bedside manner varies considerably. Basically, it boils down to one thing – a physician's ability and desire to communicate with individual patients and their caregivers. The simple fact is that most physicians don't have a good rapport with the very people that they have to explain things to. Generally, they do better bantering medical science with their colleagues because that's their comfort zone, it's the world they live in. However, when it comes down to who they really need to share information with – the patients – they often don't do it well. Rarely do they distill the information down to the point where the patients understand it. Nor are they interested in spending time to vary the conversation and use alternative approaches to reach patients and get them comfortable.

As much as physicians need to sit down and explain to patients their diseases, prognoses and treatments until they fully understand everything, the same due diligence has to happen when addressing the creative team. The reality however is that most physicians don't have the patience or the time, (not too different in the healthcare industry today). The physicians may think creative can't operate without them. And if they do, they're taking a big risk. The creative, on the other hand is hesitant to interact with medical based on many previous experiences. They simply want the process to be as painless as possible, in the vain hope their groundbreaking idea will somehow survive.

Creative Stem Cell Research.

7

Let's for a moment imagine a whole different scenario, one in which creative and medical work seamlessly together, carefully cultivating each idea to reach its full potential. In this utopian ideal, each creative tissue contains within it the precise alignment of medical relevance and creative execution that will guarantee cellular immunity – the very integrity of the idea. Picture the pristine creative concept – now as a stem cell, as pure tissue. In stem cell research the purest cell has the potential to be anything. This may be bone, central nervous system, skin, vascular or indeed anything that builds a human being. The signals that determine this outcome need to align early and precisely in the sequence to produce a refined and highly functional tissue. If not, both the integrity and functionality of the whole system could be derailed. The definition of a stem cell (in this context, an adult stem cell versus embryonic) is that it has two main properties:

1) Self-renewal or regenerative ability.
2) The capacity to differentiate.

An adult stem cell therefore has a simple agenda: *I want to create one like me. I want to make one more differentiated from myself.*

The ability for self-renewal and regeneration is to be carried out over a lifetime, so longevity is assured, (something we hope happens to creative concepts). The capacity to differentiate is related to its potency. In the creative process this ability to continually self-renew and differentiate – to campaign out – is what the Creative Clinicians call *Creative potency.* Just as in potency of stem cells, creative potency is vast and expansive at the beginning and yet able to drive self-renewal toward continued differentiation. Creative potency is defined as having the highest degree of creative potential, as preserving the idea is synonymous with what a stem cell can deliver – which is its ability to differentiate into any tissue type based on the surrounding environment, internal mediators and secondary messengers. So as the internal and external influences precisely align the creative tissue will know what it will look like and what it ultimately will become. To drive the tissue in the most compelling direction requires the right combination and the right influences of both creative and medical stakeholders so it grows into its optimal form – a marketing communication that enables a lasting, powerful emotional connection.

So, back to science; here is an adult stem cell where the world is its oyster. All it needs now is to know its purpose. Knowing the adult stem cell has the potential to be anything we have the ability to program it to be. So what exactly do we want it to do? What specific direction do we want it to go? In the marketing world, if medical/scientific and creative haven't done their research in order to program the creative stem cell properly, they're all over the map. Staying in the research of that cell longer together will certainly point it in the strongest direction necessary to sustain life. Remember, the direction a stem cell goes is one of optimal functionality and integrity. Anything shy of this steers it in a completely different direction, one that is short-lived and less functional. So to guide our creative stem cell in the right direction requires *creative stem cell research* which will ensure its creative potency. To do this means going back to the fundamental basics of both verbal and written creative briefing.

Anyone who has composed a creative brief, been part of the approval chain or even read one understands its importance. Ideally, a well-written brief should be no longer than one page and contain all the medically relevant information and inspirational material a creative team requires to conceptualize. If the creative brief is off strategy, prosaic, if the single-minded core message is muddled or can be misconstrued in any shape or form, the creative team will undoubtedly head off in the wrong direction. This ultimately results in wasted effort, time and money. Accountability at this early stage is such a critical issue. Everyone who is directly responsible for the outcome of the creative concept needs to sign off on this document. In essence, it's the research contract written out that provides the direction and purpose the creative stem cell needs. Key to the programming is that it is succinct, informative and directional. So, with every creative brief the key word is *brief,* albeit accurate. Think of the brief as an inspirational document, a launch pad for brilliant ideas, not as mental incarceration. In the best-case scenario, it will not only ensure consensus but also prove to be invaluable down the line as a foundation for a precise and protected evaluation of the creative tissues.

The Creative Clinicians believe every creative tissue has a DNA, and that the creative brief is at its very core or nucleus (as it determines the direction the tissue will ultimately go). As this cell keeps dividing, as creative tissues are cultivated, you can be sure the all-important DNA will be inherent in every one. Each will have all the necessary information packed inside that is essential for healthy growth. The DNA of the stem cell will ultimately determine how the tissue will sustain life, ensure longevity and sustain the highest level of function the longest. Here is where the precise alignment of creative and medical/science are fundamental to healthy creative tissue growth. In effect, both practices form the double helix of the DNA of the stem cell, which then sets out to program the concept or idea. Together they ensure the mapping is both medically and scientifically accurate and is the ideal platform to inspire the creative team as they begin to conceptualize. With medical and science locked into the creative and both practices joined at the hip at its inception, you can be sure the variety of opinions will drop by magnitudes. With the right balance, or meld, of creative and medical/scientific relevance few antagonists, if any, will have the status or the where-with-all to argue. Of course, to ensure a concept grows to its greatest potential you need the proper tools and processes that guarantee cellular immunity, the preservation of its integrity. So each and every concept can be optimized beginning at the level of the tissue. The Creative Clinicians call these tools and processes *Creative preventive medicine.*

Creative
Preventive Medicine.

8

Just as many diseases and conditions are either preventable or treatable, the Creative Clinicians believe the same is true of Advertitis™. Preventive creative medicine is both a philosophy and a practical approach to creating and crafting powerful marketing messages. How succinct is the creative brief? Has anything been lost in the brevity? How precisely aligned are the creative and medical/science team (the meld)? And what exactly is the difference between healthy creative tissues and those that have become inflamed and mutated? By linking these powerful diagnostic tools with the Creative Clinicians' prescriptive best practices, as creative tissues are cultivated, you can be sure each will hold the potency needed to both differentiate and thrive in challenging environments.

The Creative Clinician's MELD Evaluation

In medical practice the MELD is an acronym used in the discipline of liver transplant decision for organ donor allocation. Its purpose is simple – to more efficiently prioritize donor organs for patients on the transplant list. Each transplant candidate has a generated MELD score that is a computation utilizing a series of variables that helps establish priority for transplant based on disease severity and anticipated success of transplant. In basic terms, it's a calculated guess of potential success and need. In the case of the Creative Clinicians the MELD is a union of the medical and creative disciplines as well as a metric that leverages variables to critically assess the creative communication. These variables within the Creative Clinician MELD score are used to generate an estimate of the degree of Advertitis and impact on tissue survival. Practicing a true meld of medical and creative gives creative tissues the best chance for success along a continuum from information to distillation to visualization. The Creative Clinician MELD variables are: Medically Inspired Creative (MIC); Pharmaceutical Creative Brief (PCB 5X5); the Three-Second Idea (3-SI); Creative Aphasia (CR-A); the Six-Ball Test (6-BT); Mind-Eye Coordination (M-EC); Individual Surprise Factor (ISF); and finally Attention/Interest/Desire/Action (AIDA).

The creative MELD is a total score based on answers to YES or NO questions – 1 point for "no",

0 for "yes" – for each MELD variable. The range of lowest to highest score corresponds to the range of healthy tissue to severe Advertitis which is demonstrated by a score of 26. A score of 13 or greater is indicative of moderate-to-severe Advertitis and suggested intervention. A score of lower than 13 means Advertitis is contained and the communication is reasonably protected.

The Creative Clinician MELD score: MIC: (0-4) PCB 5X5 (0-5) 3-SI (0-2), 6-BT (0-1), M-EC (0-2), ISF (0-5), CR-A (0-2) and AIDA (0-4) AIDA tie-breaker (0-1).The range is 0-26, 0 being spot on and 26 indicating severe Advertitis

.

After familiarizing yourself with the questions that help determine the level of Advertitis, score your concept on pages 68 to 71.

Medically Inspired Creative: MIC (0-4)

Medically Inspired Creative or MIC is assessed through four questions related to white coat creative tension and creative bedside manner.

White coat creative tension:

1) Have creative and medical established a good rapport on this project?
2) Has the medical expert weighed in at the appropriate time(s) to propagate creative thinking and exploration?

Creative bedside manner:

3) Has medical sat down and explained the scientific/medical information in an engaging manner to the individual creative's level of understanding?
4) Does the creative team feel inspired by the information and key differentiators?

Pharmaceutical Creative Brief: PCB 5X5 (0-5)

In order to best maximize the power of the brief the Creative Clinicians have instigated a criterion, the PCB 5X5, to ensure everyone is literally on the same page. Employ the PCB 5X5 at the next opportunity and ask yourself and the team the following questions:

1) Does the brief present a new, inspiring perspective of the task before you?

2) Does the brief contain one clear strategic message that has a single-minded proposition as its focus?

3) Is the brief medically accurate yet written in a manner that provides a springboard for the creative mind?

4) Has the team, including the client, physically sat down and "walked" through the brief? The Creative Clinicians term this The Brief Sit Down.

5) Is the brief a binding and approved research contract that everyone who is responsible for the idea (client, account manager, strategic planner, medical director and creative director) endorsed and approved?

Three-Second Idea: 3-SI (0-2)

The Creative Clinicians believe that the life of your advertisement is only as long as it holds the reader's attention. It's therefore vital that the communication is powerful, relevant and, above all branded.

Glance at your proposed advertising communication for three seconds then answer the following questions.

1) Can you clearly repeat aloud the core message?

2) Do you remember the brand name?

If you cannot answer "yes" to both components of this question your communication is aberrant; the next tools will determine to what extent.

Six-Ball Test: 6-BT (0-1)

Numerous messages of equal parity sitting on one page inevitably fight for the customer's attention. The object of a concept is not to see how many ideas can be crammed into one communication piece, but rather how many will it endure before it ceases to be engaging. Through the Six-Ball Test, you will establish the correct hierarchy of messaging – from the most salient point (single-minded idea) down to the supporting messages (reasons to believe). Equate one ball to one marketing message.

Step 1: Throw one ball to a co-worker and have him or her catch it.

Step 2: Count the marketing messages on your tissue concept that appear to have parity and throw this number of balls to the same co-worker.

1) Could your co-worker catch all the balls at once?

If not, this is indicative of a level of Advertitis.

Mind-Eye Coordination: M-EC (0-2)

M-EC focuses on the "eye journey", the intuitive process in which your customers absorb the messages contained within an advertising communication. Each communication will contain a number of elements, eg, headline, visual, a combined headline and visual, subhead, eyebrow and tagline. The customer has to be able to easily scan them in a way that makes sense from a story flow perspective. With this in mind answer the following questions.

1) Is the communication constructed in a way that easily directs your attention to connect to the primary element (the single-minded idea) and then to its secondary elements?

2) Was the communication clear and precise?

If the answer is "no" to these questions, this is indicative of an inflamed and swollen ad. Ensure your and your customers' attention are immediately grabbed by the single-minded idea and then that it intuitively follows through on the hierarchy of message points.

Individual Surprise Factor: ISF (0-5)

The way in which we view information is largely based on existing or established beliefs. After studying ads in the category is there anything that *you* find unique? Something you haven't typically seen before, eg, color, shape? Claim? Or maybe you saw something that wasn't physically there. With these points in mind answer the following questions.

1) Was there a compelling, unexpected element or intriguing twist that surprised you?

2) Was there an unexpected or refreshing approach in a category full of predictable imagery or text?

3) Do you remember the advertisement several days or more afterwards?

4) Did you experience a gastromonic sensation (ie, gut reaction)?

5) Did you experience feelings of envy or fear (eg, why didn't my agency come up with it? My brand is going to tank!)?

Creative Aphasia: CR-A (0-2)

Creative aphasia is defined as the loss of a previously held ability to communicate effectively.

Broca's advertisement:
1) Does the ad communicate anything to you?

Wernicke's advertisement:
2) Is the ad communicating a focused and comprehensible message in an effortless way?

Attention/Interest/Desire/Action: AIDA (0-4)

The following four steps on the AIDA scale are essential to a successful marketing communication.

Attention: 1) Will the ad immediately grab my customer's attention?

Interest: 2) Does it pique my customer's interest and have at its heart a relevant, single-minded differentiating proposition?

Desire: 3) Is the competitive differentiator big enough to persuade my customer to seriously consider changing a prescribing behavior?

Action: 4) Will the compelling proposition embed itself into the customer's mind so he or she takes decisive action at the point of purchase?

Breaking the Tie Between '*I*' and '*D*'. (0-1)

Moving your customer from interest to desire is paramount. Desire means something resonates deeply and it intricately matters. When this happens, you've moved your customer from *this has piqued my interest* to *this will change my life and the lives of my patients in a positive manner*. Whatever the desire is it will certainly involve strong rational and emotional components. The following question is the tie-breaker.

5) Was "yes" the answer to the third question above?

Medically Inspired Creative: MIC

	Yes(0)	No(1)
1) Have creative and medical established a good rapport on this project?		
2) Has the medical expert weighed in at the appropriate time(s) to propagate creative thinking and exploration?		
3) Has medical sat down and explained the scientific/medical information in an engaging manner to the individual creative's level of understanding?		
4) Does the creative team feel inspired by the information and key differentiators?		
Subtotal		

Pharmaceutical Creative Brief: PCB 5X5

	Yes(0)	No(1)
1) Does the brief present a new, inspiring perspective of the task before you?		
2) Does the brief contain one clear strategic message that has a single-minded proposition as its focus?		
3) Is the brief medically accurate yet written in a manner that provides a springboard for the creative mind?		
4) Has the team, including the client, physically sat down and "walked" through the brief?		
5) Is the brief a binding and approved research contract that everyone who is responsible for the idea (client, account manager, strategic planner, medical director and creative director) endorsed and approved?		
Subtotal		

	Yes(0)	No(1)
Three-Second Idea: 3-SI		
1) Can you clearly repeat aloud the core message?		
2) Do you remember the brand name?		
Subtotal		
Six-Ball Test: 6-BT		
1) Could your co-worker catch all the balls at once?		
Subtotal		
Mind-Eye Coordination: M-EC		
1) Is the communication constructed in a way that easily directs your attention to connect to the primary element (the single-minded idea) and then to its secondary elements?		
2) Was the communication clear and precise?		
Subtotal		

Individual Surprise Factor: ISF

	Yes(0)	No(1)
1) Was there a compelling, unexpected element or intriguing twist that surprised you?		
2) Was there an unexpected or refreshing approach in a category full of predictable imagery or text?		
3) Do you remember the advertisement several days or more afterwards?		
4) Did you experience a gastromonic sensation (ie, gut reaction)?		
5) Did you experience feelings of envy or fear (eg, why didn't my agency come up with it? My brand is going to tank!)?		
Subtotal		

Creative Aphasia: CR-A

	Yes(0)	No(1)
1) Does the ad communicate anything to you?		
2) Is the ad communicating a focussed and comprehensible message in an effortless way?		
Subtotal		

AIDA. Attention/Interest/Desire/Action	Yes(0)	No(1)
Attention: 1) Will the ad immediately grab my customer's attention?		
Interest: 2) Does it pique my customer's interest and have at its heart a relevant, single-minded differentiating proposition?		
Desire: 3) Is the competitive differentiator big enough to persuade my customer to seriously consider changing a prescribing behavior?		
Action: 4) Will the compelling proposition embed itself into the customer's mind so he or she takes decisive action at the point of purchase?		
Tie breaker: 5) Was "yes" the answer to the third question above?		
Subtotal		
Total		

Of the eight creative MELD categories presented on the previous pages, the Creative Clinicians have identified four that critically assess and emphasize the importance of strong medical and creative collaboration.

These are the M-EC, PCB 5X5, MIC and CR-A. Together they represent 13 points, or half of the highest possible score of 26 (indicating severe Advertitis).

By tapping into the power of the creative MELD and optimizing the collaboration of medical and creative right from the outset, you will be able to minimize any significant degree of Advertitis, thereby ensuring your advertising message has the best possible chance for success.

1	13	26

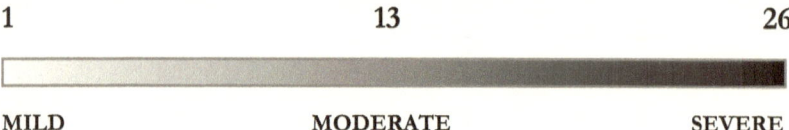

MILD	MODERATE	SEVERE

The Creative Clinician's Top 10 Pharma Advertising Clichés.

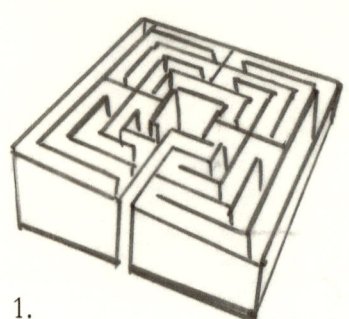

1.

2.

3.

4.

5.

6.

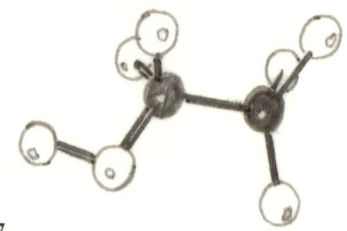

7

Ten tired clichés that anyone evaluating the creative tissue should immediately reject.

8.

9.

10.

1. The maze.

2. Arms aloft in triumph.

3. Timepieces.

4. Happy smiling patient.

5. Jigsaws and games.

6. Boxing gloves.

7. The high science story.

8. Road signs.

9. Cartoon organs.

10. Medical menagerie on skateboards etcetera.

A prognosis for healthcare advertising.

9

Our industry's integrity is in jeopardy, it has been for a while now, and rather ironically the finger of blame points to success. As success built over time and people realized how much money could be made, creative advertising was succeeded by audacious claims that became difficult to deliver on. It was all about instant gratification. We had to feed the beast we all got used to having. Even when the blockbuster pipeline dried to a trickle, big pharma kept on rolling the only way it knew how – by acquisition, (where's the ingenuity in that?). Somewhere along the way it stopped being about the patient and good medicine and became more about cold, hard profit and loss. Today, the noise is more important than the actual craft. And not surprisingly, two very important groups have brought the industry sharply under the microscope. First of all, the public who are tired of false hope and lies. And secondly, the FDA and government bodies that perhaps understandably have taken a harder road of control and pulled on the reins because of the inflammatory nature of many claims. (The most commonly cited violation to date in 2009 is omission/minimization of safety/risk information.)

Position by Imposition

Yet as swiftly as the FDA dishes out the mandates and slaps the wrists (as well as the writs), the deluge of warnings has fallen on some very noncompliant, unsympathetic ears. Recently, a prominent CEO stated that the only reason his company had to put any appropriate use or regulatory guidance (REMs) criteria around their product was because of the class. He argued the baggage of other products was the reason behind it – in other words just a formality. Not surprisingly, the FDA came down like a judge's gavel. Rather tersely they pointed out that it wasn't because of the class but for the simple reason that the product data sent up a number of red flags. Of course, the CEO in question wasn't going out on a limb – far from it. Like so many others he adopted a *position as imposition*. In other words, *you can't tell me what to do. You are imposing on me so my position on this is that it's position by imposition.*

As obvious as it sounds, the FDA is creating our

world and we have to live in it. The signals are all there
– you think the tidal wave can be stopped? The breeze
is already here. We have to start producing advertising
that falls within the government and FDA guidelines –
to the letter, (not the violation kind). Yes, it is about
fitting in. However, we as marketers can also say there is
a unique opportunity to be far more articulate and
compelling than the industry is currently being. It's our
duty to deliver brilliant creative – to effect change and
bring the credibility and trust back to the industry,
because at the end of the day, the one who ultimately
suffers is the end-user – the patient.

From Camouflage to Transparency

Today, with so many products designed for specific
populations success has to be built slowly and steadily
based on fundamentals. It's an endurance test – a very
finessed step-by-step approach. Ten years ago around
twenty products in the pipeline were biologics. Now
there's two to three thousand. That's mind-boggling!
Science is going into genetic architecture, single nuclear
polymorphisms (or SNP) and becoming so microscoped into personalized medicine that if our industry
as it stands isn't controlled some kind of Pandora's box
will be opened. Advancements in science are going at a
more rapid pace than the environment can adapt to. So,
crucial to success will be introducing products in a
responsible manner apposite to where the industry's

current standing in the global community. If we uphold our primary duty, to make sure the patient is safe, the benefits will surely follow. By leveraging our expertise in medicine and creative we can bring about more powerful messages than ever before. We need to rise to this challenge and push ourselves professionally to unveil brilliant and compelling creative within a more rigorous framework and environment of intense scrutiny. This is a different kind of success, one based on the fundamentals and built to regain trust. Recreate what you believe trust is and trust itself becomes the transition. By embracing the trends we move from camouflage to transparency and in doing so people will again say the pharmaceutical industry has my best interest in mind. Now doesn't that sound like a win-win scenario?

Bring Back the Passion

Of course, what's happening is hardly a new phenomenon – it's a cyclic pattern. In 1994, the Major League Baseball strike got so bad that fans were leaving the stands in droves. Something had to be done to turn the situation around and the answer was simple – integrity. Once integrity came into play it was all about the game again. The industry got the passion back. Suddenly, it was about the squeeze play, triple play – the slide – the steal and the home run. This is what that baseball was designed to be. Well, in the same way baseball got its passion back – so can we. Let's face it, the patients aren't cheering for anything – and somehow we have to get them back on the side of the pharmaceutical industry so they enjoy the benefit of a greater quality of life. To bring the passion back requires a back-to-basics approach – look to the fundamentals, do the due diligence and keep things in check. The future is assured if we have the fundamentals of passion, professionalism, ethics and legality. If we can get to the fundamentals that preserve great thinking, then the passion will come.

The Potency in What We Can Say.

As pharmaceutical marketing moves forward into the ever-challenging field of microscoped personalized medicine, there will be precious little room for maneuvering. So, it's essential that our ideas are as potent as they can be. Let's go back to the idea of a stem cell. The most effective and efficient way is to judiciously employ creative stem cell research, preserve the tissue and do something that is going to stand the test of time. Start with the purity of the tissue idea, realize its full potential – and *then* differentiate across our market. To have the creative potency – the ability to maximize infinite potential yet also differentiate is the whole essence of adult stem cell research.

We hope that you, like us, see an exciting time full of challenges and opportunities. Embracing the future, rekindling the passion, preserving the tissue and avoiding Advertitis will ultimately lead to new, more inventive, medically relevant solutions. The time of one-upmanship has passed. And to be perfectly honest, there aren't many creative advertising avenues left other than a mutation of the very clichéd imagery that so prolifically breed in the marketing materials. Much like the pharmaceutical industry, our creativity has become compromised, and it's perhaps not so surprising that Advertitis has escalated to such epidemic proportions. The way it's going, that ubiquitous animal on the skateboard may just have to become two-headed – just to get ahead!

Creative Clinician's Grand Rounds.

Birth of a Notion

Today's pharmaceutical advertising is in the most fundamental sense an often-confusing mix of messages and claims with little priority in terms of importance.

Without an innate connection between the two skills sets (medical and creative), truly compelling, medically relevant creative solutions will continue to be elusive.

Why 'Itis'?

If a best-practice process is not followed routinely, there is a lack of compliance or poor use of the tools available to help guide the creative work.

Anyone working in pharmaceutical marketing will testify to the frustration, systematic pushback and various immovable stances taken by all stakeholders. This slow, progressive infectious process inflames the creative tissue to such a degree that the very integrity of the idea is lost.

The Detail That Goes Into Saying Nothing

There is now an almost frantic need to make the concepts *more correct*. In fact, making the concepts *more correct* has become the whole goal!

By the time the advertisement reaches the medical journals, it will be a perplexing mess of countless message points. Paralysis from the headline down, eyebrows, subheads and tag lines will grapple for the reader's attention.

The Silent Killer

If you haven't some framework of immunity then anyone can attack your creative tissue.

There is the Broca's advertisement, where the result is that the ad is saying absolutely nothing to the customer. Then there's the Wernicke's advertisement where the ad is saying innumerable things but nothing is being expressed.

Similarly to chronic HCV, where the organ is damaged before any outward signs are recognized, the processes within pharmaceutical advertising have slowly, over time been damaging the functionality of its communications.

The big question is how are we going to make sure the creative solution embraces the challenges within healthcare so it resonates with where we're going?

Harley Street Meets Sesame Street

Any successful pharmaceutical concept is a meld of both medical relevance and creative interpretation.

Both creative and medical need to set expectations together, understand the past and develop a way of communicating as one solid partnership.

As much as physicians need to sit down and explain to patients their diseases, prognoses and treatments until they fully understand everything, the same due diligence has to happen when addressing the creative team.

Creative Stem Cell Research

In the creative process, this ability to continually self-renew and differentiate – to campaign out – is what the Creative Clinicians call *Creative potency*.

Creative potency is defined as having the highest degree of creative potential, as preserving the idea is synonymous with what a stem cell can deliver – which is its ability to differentiate into any tissue type based on the surrounding environment, internal mediators and secondary messengers.

The Creative Stem Cell

To drive the tissue in the most compelling direction requires the right combination and the right influences of both creative and medical stakeholders so it grows into its optimal form – a marketing communication that enables a lasting, powerful emotional connection.

To guide our creative stem cell in the right direction requires *creative stem cell research*, which will ensure its creative potency.

A Prognosis for Healthcare Advertising

As pharmaceutical marketing moves forward into the ever-challenging field of microscoped personalized medicine, there will be precious little room for maneuvering.

We believe that by embracing the future, rekindling the passion, preserving the tissue and avoiding Advertitis will ultimately lead to new, more inventive, medically relevant solutions.

Share it with others

You can order copies of Advertitis™
at amazon.com
To enquire about Advertitis™ Training Materials go to:
advertitis.com

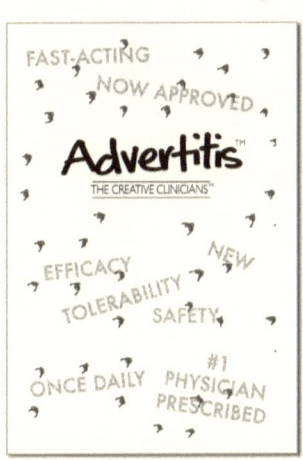

Concerned that your advertising ideas may be suffering
from Advertitis™?
Have ever-stricter regulatory guidance limitations and
mandates ever suffocated any compelling communication?
The book, tools and workshops offered up by
The Creative Clinicians™ pave the way for brilliant medically
inspired creative in an environment ever-governed under a
microscope of scrutiny.

About the Authors

Craig Sponseller, M.D., has more than a decade of experience in direct patient care first as an internist and then subsequently as a subspecialist in gastroenterology, hepatology and transplantation. As a physician and healthcare communications expert, he has worked with more than 20 global pharmaceutical clients across a range of therapeutic categories in the capacity of medical strategist and Chief Medical Officer in both independent and corporate holding companies. He is an expert at blending and elevating clinical insights to ensure brand success. Dr. Sponseller is published in both peer review medical journals and pharmaceutical advertising.

Ross Thomson's career in both consumer and pharma advertising spans nearly three decades. Roles as both copywriter and Creative Director include Publicis London, McCann-Erickson and other major UK agencies. In 2004, he moved to New York City as Chief Creative Officer Worldwide of Grey Healthcare Group, where he and his team consistently won gold and silver in every major pharma advertising award scheme. Agencies and clients alike, notably, Pfizer, Wyeth, Genentech, GSK and Forest have all greatly benefited from Ross's creative evaluation workshops. An avid writer, he is a regular contributor to pharmaceutical marketing magazines.

www.ingramcontent.com/pod-product-compliance
Lightning Source LLC
Chambersburg PA
CBHW030346290526
45785CB00004B/1619